☙ PROFILES OF GREAT ❧
BLACK AMERICANS

Performing
Artists

☙❧

Edited by Richard Rennert
Introduction by Coretta Scott King

||| A Chelsea House
||| Multibiography

Chelsea House Publishers
New York   Philadelphia

920
REN

5   7   9   8   6   4

Library of Congress Cataloging-in-Publication Data

Performing artists/edited by Richard Rennert.
p. cm.—(Profiles of great Black Americans)
Includes bibliographical references and index.
ISBN   0-7910-2069-X.
            0-7910-2070-3 (pbk.)
    1. Afro-American entertainers—Biography—Juvenile
literature. 2. Afro-Americans in the performing arts—Juvenile
literature. [1. Entertainers. 2. Afro-Americans—Biography.]
I. Rennert, Richard Scott, 1956– . II. Series.
PN2286.P44 1993   93-25674
791'.08996073—dc20   CIP
[B]   AC

☙ CONTENTS ❧

❧ INTRODUCTION ❧
by Coretta Scott King

This book is about black Americans who served society through the excellence of their achievements. It forms a part of the rich history of black men and women in America—a history of stunning accomplishments in every field of human endeavor, from literature and art to science, industry, education, diplomacy, athletics, jurisprudence, even polar exploration.

Not all of the people in this history had the same ideals, but I think you will find something that all of them had in common. Like Martin Luther King, Jr., they all decided to become "drum majors" and serve humanity. In that principle—whether it was expressed in books, inventions, or song—they found something outside themselves to use as a goal and a guide. Something that showed them a way to serve others, instead of only living for themselves.

Reading the stories of these courageous men and women not only helps us discover the principles that we will use to guide our own lives but also teaches us about our black heritage and about America itself. It is crucial for us to know the heroes and heroines of our history and to realize that the price we paid in our struggle for equality in America was dear. But we must also understand that we have gotten as far as we have partly because America's democratic system and ideals made it possible.

We are still struggling with racism and prejudice. But the great men and women in this series are a tribute to the spirit of our democratic ideals and the system in which they have flourished. And that makes their stories special and worth knowing.

ALVIN AILEY

Choreographer and director Alvin Ailey, Jr., was born on January 5, 1931, in Rogers, Texas. He was the only child of Alvin Ailey, a laborer, and his wife, Lula. When Alvin junior was very young, his parents separated, and he was raised by his mother. In 1942, Mrs. Ailey and her son moved to Los Angeles.

Alvin was active in school sports and also took tap dancing lessons. Another early influence was the ritual of the Báptist church, which fascinated Alvin, and he was also drawn to that form of African American music known as the blues. In 1948, following his graduation from high school, Alvin enrolled briefly at the University of California, Los Angeles (UCLA), then transferred to Los Angeles City College, where he remained until 1951.

Two years earlier, in 1949, Ailey had been introduced to the work of Lester Horton, an African American modern-dance choreographer, and began attending weekend classes offered by Horton. By 1951, Ailey was serving on the stage crew of the Lester Horton Dance Theater and also dancing with Horton's company. Yet he was still not fully committed to a career in dancing and made plans to become a teacher. He moved to San Francisco and enrolled at San Francisco State College as a student of Romance languages. The lure of dancing proved too strong, however, and by early 1953 Ailey was dancing in a nightclub act in San Francisco. In May of that year, he returned to Los Angeles and rejoined the Lester Horton Dance Theater.

Six months later, in November 1953, Horton died, and a committee was formed to keep the company together. Ailey began choreographing dances for the group and two of them, *Mourning Morning* and *According to St. Francis*, were performed at the world-famous Jacob's Pillow Dance Festival in the summer of 1954. That same year Ailey danced in the film *Carmen Jones* and was invited to appear in the Broadway production of *House of Flowers*, a musical written by Truman Capote, which opened in December 1954.

Following his move to New York City, Ailey studied dance with many well-known choreographers, including Martha Graham. He appeared in other musicals, including *The Carefree Tree* (1955) and Harry Belafonte's *Sing, Man, Sing* (1956). In 1957, he became the leading dancer in *Jamaica*, a musical that starred Lena Horne.

In March 1958, Ailey and fellow dancer-choreographer Ernest Parham assembled a group of dancers, most of them from the cast of *Jamaica*, and presented a program at the 92nd Street YMHA in New York City. For this presentation, Ailey choreographed three pieces: *Ode and Homage* (to Lester Horton), *Blues Suite*, and five dances with Latin themes that were later retitled *Cinco Latinos*. Ailey was widely praised for both his choreography and his dancing and soon afterward he formed the Alvin Ailey American Dance Theater, a troupe of both black and white dancers that gave its first full-scale concert in December 1958 at the YMHA.

As Ailey's reputation grew, he continued to dance and to choreograph new works. *Revelations*, widely considered his masterwork, premiered at the YMHA in January 1960. According to the program notes, *Revelations* explored the "motivations and emotions of American Negro religious music." It was an instant hit and was later included in every presentation by the Alvin Ailey Dance Theater.

In the fall of 1960, Ailey presented his first program at the Clark Center for the Performing Arts, which was part of New York City's West Side YWCA. The Clark Center soon became the headquarters of the Alvin Ailey Dance Theater. Rehearsals were conducted there, and dance classes were offered. At his Clark Center performances, Ailey began including the works of other choreographers in his repertory, a practice that was generally not followed by other modern-dance companies. Ailey revived Lester Horton's *The Beloved* and presented the New York premiere of choreographer Joan Butler's *Portrait of Billie*, a dance about jazz singer Billie Holiday.

In 1960–61, Ailey also introduced a new work of his own, *Knoxville: Summer of 1915*, choreographed to music by Samuel Barber, and a duet, *Roots of the Blues*, which he danced with Carmen de Lavallade. The duet premiered at the Boston Arts Festival in June 1961 and was presented later that summer in concert at Lewisohn Stadium in New York City. In December of that year, Ailey introduced another work that was soon widely acclaimed: *Hermit Songs*, again set to music by Samuel Barber, and featuring Ailey in a solo role.

In February 1962, Ailey and codirector Carmen de Lavallade led the company on a tour of the Far East sponsored by the U.S. State Department. The group visited 10 countries and presented a number of what had now become modern-dance classics, including *Been Here and Gone*, Ailey's suite of African American folk dances, and Glen Tetley's *Mountain Way Chant*, based on Navajo Indian rituals. The tour marked the first time an African American company had performed in Southeast Asia, and audiences responded enthusiastically, especially in Australia. The company's warm reception established their reputation as a group with universal appeal and paved the way for future international tours.

During the summer of 1962, the Alvin Ailey Dance Theater performed at the American Dance Festival in New London, Connecticut. Ailey also created new dances for the Robert Joffrey Ballet, including the famous *Feast of Ashes*, which later became part of the repertory of the Harkness Ballet. In September, the Ailey company appeared twice at a dance festival held in New York's Central Park.

During the next few years, Ailey taught dance classes at the Clark Center and toured with his company throughout the United States, appearing mostly on college and university campuses. In 1963, Ailey introduced *Labyrinth*, based on the myth of Theseus and the Minotaur; the work was subsequently revised and became his well-known ballet *Ariadne*. Also in 1963, Ailey and his company appeared at the Century of Negro Progress exhibit in Chicago, where their fellow performers included Duke Ellington. That fall the Alvin Ailey Dance Theater traveled to Brazil, where they performed at the Music and Dance Festival in Rio de Janeiro.

In the fall of 1964, the Ailey company embarked on its first tour of London and the continent of Europe. Enthusiastic audiences cheered every performance—

in Hamburg the group received an unprecedented 61 curtain calls—and critics raved. In December, the company revisited Australia, and in the spring of 1965 returned to London for more appearances. By the end of that year, Ailey was no longer performing, but he continued to direct the group and to choreograph new dances. In the early 1960s, he also appeared as an actor in several off-Broadway plays.

In 1966, Ailey traveled with his dance company to Dakar, Senegal, where they appeared at the World Festival of the Negro Arts—the first racially in-tegrated group to do so. Later that spring they ap-peared with the Harkness Ballet in Barcelona and Paris. In addition to work for his own company that year, Ailey choreographed the dances for *Antony and Cleopatra*, the opera by Samuel Barber that opened the new Metropolitan Opera House in New York City in September 1966.

During the following two decades, Ailey main-tained his troupe's prominence as the most popular modern-dance group in the world. His later works included *Masekela Language* (1969), *Cry* (1971), and *Night Creature* (1974), one of several homages to Duke Ellington. Ailey died in New York City on December 1, 1989.

Singer Marian Anderson was born in Philadelphia, Pennsylvania, sometime around 1900. She always claimed that her birth date was February 1902, but toward the end of her life newly discovered family documents indicated that she had been born on February 27, 1897. Her father, John Anderson, sold ice and coal at the Reading Terminal Market in downtown Philadelphia. Marian began singing in public at the age of six, when she joined the choir at the Union Baptist Church, which her family attended.

Marian Anderson's father died when she was 10 years old, and the family moved in with her paternal grandparents. Her mother supported Marian and her two younger sisters by working as a cleaning woman in a department store. When Marian was 14, the famous black tenor Roland Hayes performed at the Union Baptist Church and Marian was asked by the choir director to appear on the same program. Hayes was astonished by the quality of the young woman's voice and encouraged her to get further training.

Encouraged by Hayes's opinion of her voice, Marian realized that she might be able to help support her family by singing professionally, but she still needed additional training. At the age of 15 she tried to enroll in a small music school in Philadelphia but was rejected because of her race. Despite her lack of formal singing lessons, her reputation grew and she was hired to sing at church socials and benefits in the black community.

When Anderson was a junior in high school, a family friend introduced her to a black voice teacher named Mary Patterson, who agreed to give her free lessons. Anderson progressed rapidly, and when she graduated from high school, the principal, Dr. Lucy Wilson, arranged for her to audition with an Italian vocal coach named Giuseppe Boghetti. After Boghetti agreed to accept her as a pupil, Dr. Wilson and the

Union Baptist Church arranged a benefit concert to raise money for voice lessons. Roland Hayes performed and the event raised more than $600, enough for a year of lessons. Although Boghetti remained her teacher for many years, he never charged her for lessons after the first year.

Through her studies with Boghetti, Anderson expanded her repertoire and was now performing more frequently, sometimes two or three times in the same evening. She soon found an accompanist named Billy King, and he became her manager. Anderson and King became well known in Philadelphia and were much in demand; within two years they were being paid $100 for each performance. In 1920, Anderson embarked on her first tour, performing with King at black colleges throughout the South before returning to Philadelphia for more concerts.

In 1923, Anderson competed in a vocal contest sponsored by the Philharmonic Society of Philadelphia and became the first black singer to win. Her prize was an invitation to perform with the Philadelphia Orchestra in a concert that was broadcast over the radio. Later that same year she sang in a standing-room-only concert in New York City's Harlem, followed by several other appearances in the city.

In April 1924, Anderson gave a major recital at New York's Town Hall before a largely white audience. Applause was polite but restrained, and critics panned her performance, especially her "wooden" rendering of songs in German. A dejected Anderson returned to

Philadelphia and several months passed before she resumed her singing.

In 1925, after intensive study with Boghetti, Anderson entered a competition sponsored by the National Music League in New York City. Following an arduous selection process, Anderson was declared the winner. Her prize was an appearance with the New York Philharmonic that summer at Lewisohn Stadium, an enormous open-air theater in the city.

The concert was a resounding success and critics praised Anderson for her remarkable voice. Invitations for her to perform came pouring in from around the country. That fall she toured Canada and California with King, and other engagements followed as her fees rose to as much as $500 per concert. While King continued as her accompanist, she acquired a new manager, Arthur Judson, the head of a prestigious concert bureau in New York.

Despite her successes during the next few years, Anderson believed that she needed training abroad to improve her singing and language skills. In the summer of 1929, she traveled to England, where she studied voice for several months and performed at London's Wigmore Hall. Two years later, supported by a grant from the Julius Rosenwald Fund, Anderson sailed for Germany. Boarding with a family in Berlin to improve her German, she took voice lessons and gave a recital at the Bachsaal, a celebrated music hall in the city. Before returning to America in 1932, Anderson gave a series of concerts in Scandinavia that were well received.

In 1933, Anderson traveled again to Europe with the assistance of another grant from the Rosenwald Fund. She made a second tour of Scandinavia, giving 108 concerts in other European cities, including Paris, Geneva, Brussels, Vienna, and Salzburg, which had been arranged for her by the Judson agency. In Paris, she was heard by the noted American impresario Sol Hurok, who offered her a new contract upon her return to the United States. In the audience at her Salzburg concert was the renowned conductor Arturo Toscanini, who came backstage afterward and told her that "Yours is a voice one hears once in a hundred years."

Anderson came back to the United States in December 1935 with a new accompanist, the Finnish pianist Kosti Vehanen. On December 30, she returned to New York City's Town Hall to present a concert arranged for her by Sol Hurok. This time the audience and critics alike were wildly enthusiastic—despite the fact that Anderson performed with a broken ankle. She had injured herself in a fall on board ship a week earlier, but her cast was carefully concealed by her long gown.

Anderson returned to Europe in March 1936 for further concerts, again accompanied by Vehanen. The highlight of the tour was a series of engagements in the Soviet Union, one of which was attended by dictator Joseph Stalin. During the next few years, Anderson and Vehanen toured in the United States, Europe, and South America. She was now internationally acclaimed, and many honors were bestowed upon her. In 1936, she became the first black singer to perform at the White House, at the invitation of President and Mrs. Franklin D. Roosevelt. In 1938, she received an honorary doctorate in music from Howard University in Washington, D.C., the first of dozens of honorary degrees that she would be awarded during her lifetime. In January 1939, Anderson was named the recipient of the Spingarn Medal, an honor conferred annually by the National Association for the Advancement of Colored People (NAACP) for "the highest or noblest achievement by an American Negro."

The year 1939 also brought Marian Anderson an experience that made headlines around the world. When Sol Hurok tried to book Anderson for a concert at Constitution Hall in Washington, D.C., he learned that the owners of the hall, a patriotic organization called the Daughters of the American Revolution, excluded black performers from appearing there. An outraged Hurok informed the press about the ban and support for Anderson poured in from around the country. Many famous Americans publicly criticized the DAR's policy, and First Lady Eleanor Roosevelt resigned from the organization in protest.

The Roosevelts and Secretary of the Interior Harold Ickes came to the rescue by inviting Anderson to give a free public recital on the steps of the Lincoln Memorial on Easter Sunday, April 9, 1939. Anderson, who had remained calm and dignified throughout the uproar and refused to comment publicly on the DAR's decision, accepted the government's offer and gave a memorable concert that was attended by 75,000 people. Four years later, when the DAR invited her to sing at a benefit concert at Constitution Hall, she graciously agreed to perform.

Anderson, now an international superstar, continued to give concerts throughout the world, accompanied by a new pianist, a German refugee named Franz Rupp, after Vehanen returned to Finland in 1940. During World War II, she made frequent tours of military bases, entertaining troops. In 1943, she married Orpheus Fisher, an architect whom she had first met in 1922. They bought a farm near Danbury, Connecticut, and Fisher built his wife a separate studio where she could practice undisturbed.

In 1955, Anderson reached another milestone in her career when she became the first black singer to perform with the Metropolitan Opera in New York City, singing the role of the sorceress Ulrica in Verdi's *A Masked Ball.* Her acclaimed performance opened the door for other black singers at the Metropolitan Opera, including Leontyne Price. In January 1957, she sang "The Star-Spangled Banner" at President Dwight D. Eisenhower's inauguration and later that year made a worldwide goodwill tour at the request of the U.S. State Department. In 1958–59, she served as a member of the U.S. delegation to the United Nations, and in January 1961, she sang at the inauguration of President John F. Kennedy. Three years later she was awarded the Presidential Medal of Freedom by President Lyndon B. Johnson.

Anderson, accompanied by Franz Rupp, gave her final concert on April 19, 1965—Easter Sunday—at Carnegie Hall. This was the climax of a farewell tour that had begun the previous October at Constitution Hall in Washington, D.C. In retirement, she continued her involvement in the artistic life of the country, participating in numerous musical and charitable organizations and receiving countless honors, including a lifetime achievement award from the Kennedy Center for the Performing Arts in Washington, D.C., in 1978.

In 1992, Anderson moved from her Connecticut home to Portland, Oregon, to live with her nephew, James De Priest, the conductor of the Oregon Symphony. She died in Portland on April 8, 1993.

Singer and dancer Josephine Baker was born Josephine McDonald in St. Louis, Missouri, on June 3, 1906, the oldest of three children. Her father was an itinerant musician who was seldom at home, and her mother supported the family by taking in laundry. Josephine was an imaginative child who enjoyed dressing up in adult clothes and giving "plays" in the family's basement.

Between the ages of 8 and 10 she stayed out of school in order to earn money as a kitchen helper, maid, and baby-sitter. She later recalled that she was not especially happy in elementary school anyway, since she was constantly being reprimanded by her teachers for making faces.

By the time she was a teenager, Josephine had moved to Philadelphia, where she lived for a while with her grandmother. She had been married briefly at the age of 13 in St. Louis and two years later married Willie Baker, a Pullman porter. Josephine frequently attended local vaudeville shows and began dancing in a chorus line. At the age of 16 she joined a traveling troupe of dancers and by 1923 was dancing in New York City in a musical comedy called *Shuffle*. Her improvisation and mimicry drew such applause that she was hired to do another show, *Chocolate Dandies*, on Broadway. When that closed, Baker joined the floor show at the Plantation Club at $125 a week.

In 1925, Baker, who was now separated from her second husband, was offered a major dancing role in an American-sponsored French show, *La Revue Nègre*, at twice her Plantation Club salary. The production opened at the Théâtre des Champs-Elysées in Paris that fall and introduced what the French called *le jazz hot* to Europe. Baker was an instant success and was soon hired away by the celebrated Folies Bergère, Paris's most famous music hall. Here she was billed as "Dark Star" and created a sensation by dancing on a mirror, clothed only in a bunch of rubber bananas strung around her waist. Banana-clad Josephine dolls were soon being sold on the streets of Paris to thousands of children and tourists.

In December 1926, while still performing at the Folies Bergère, Baker founded her own nightclub, Chez Josephine, on the rue Pigalle; it was later moved to the rue Fontaine and finally to rue François I. By this time Baker was wealthy and famous, and had acquired a reputation as a charming eccentric who often walked her pet leopards down the Champs-Elysées, the main thoroughfare of Paris. She received thousands of fan letters, many of them proposing marriage. From 1928 to 1930, she toured the world and performed in 25 countries.

In 1930, Baker's manager and close friend, Pepito Abatino, persuaded her to talk and sing during her performances. The director of the Casino de Paris, Henri Varna, created a new show for Baker, and she left the Folies Bergère briefly to make her formal debut that fall as a singing and dancing comedienne at the Casino. Critics and audiences raved at Baker's transformation from an exotic dancer into "a complete artist, the perfect master of her tools."

Returning to the Folies Bergère, Baker found her name in neon lights on the marquee and giant color photographs of her flanking the entrance. Throughout the 1930s, she continued as the star attraction at the Folies while appearing in movies and light opera. Her film debut occurred in the summer of 1934 when she appeared as the title character in *Zouzou*, the story of a laundress who becomes a music hall star. In December 1934, she began a six-month run at the Theâtre Marigny as the star of *La Creole*, an operetta about a Jamaican girl that was based on music by Jacques Offenbach. Baker made several more films during the 1930s. In 1937, following a divorce from Willie Baker, she married for a third time; her new husband was a millionaire businessman named Jean Lyon. That same year Baker became a French citizen. She and Lyon separated several years later.

When German troops invaded Belgium in May 1940, Baker became a Red Cross volunteer, helping fleeing Belgian refugees. The next month, following the German takeover of France, Baker joined the underground intelligence network and carried secret messages from the Italian embassy to a French army captain named Jacques Abtey. In October, Baker, accompanied by Abtey, began a journey that took her on secret missions to London, Spain, Portugal, and finally to Rio de Janeiro, Brazil, where she performed in several shows. Returning to Marseilles in December 1940, she appeared in a revival of *La Creole*. Early the following year she traveled to Algiers, North Africa, and remained there to recuperate from severe bronchitis.

Beginning in early 1942, Baker traveled throughout North Africa and the Middle East entertaining troops. She was officially designated as a sublieutenant in the women's auxiliary of the Free French forces, and after the war ended she was honored by the French government with the Legion of Honor and the Rosette of the Resistance.

Following the liberation of Paris in August 1944, Baker returned to the French capital and starred in a revue at the Théâtre aux Armées. In the postwar years Baker alternated appearances at the Folies Bergère with frequent world tours. She appeared occasionally on French television and also recorded several well-known songs from her repertoire, including "Pretty Little Baby" and "J'Ai Deux Amours." In 1947, she married her fourth and last husband, Jo Bouillon, a French orchestra leader.

During these years, Baker also became increasingly involved with the development of her 300-acre country estate in southwest France, where she kept numerous pet animals.

The centerpiece of the estate was a medieval chateau named Les Milandes, which she had begun renting in the 1930s and eventually purchased outright. In the early 1950s, Baker began adopting orphaned babies of various nationalities and raising them at the estate.

In 1956, Baker announced her retirement from show business and became a full-time resident of Les Milandes to preside over what she called her rainbow family, which eventually numbered 12 children. However, the cost of running Les Milandes forced her to return to the Paris stage three years later in *Paris, Mes Amours*, a musical based on her own life. The following year she took the show on a world tour.

Beginning in the 1930s, Baker had returned several times to the United States to perform before American audiences. Following a visit in the early 1950s, during which she was the target of racial snubs,

Baker was openly critical of America's treatment of blacks. In August 1963, she traveled to Washington, D.C., to participate in the March on Washington, the civil rights demonstration that featured Martin Luther King, Jr., delivering his famous "I have a dream" speech. Two months later Baker came to New York City and gave a benefit performance for the civil rights movement at Carnegie Hall.

In early 1964, Baker presented shows at the Brooks Atkinson and Henry Miller theaters in New York City. After her return to Les Milandes that spring, she spent much of her time trying to keep her "experiment in brotherhood" from falling into financial ruin. The strain on her health was enormous, and in July she suffered a severe heart attack, followed by a second one three months later. As she recuperated during the next few years, Baker still sought to save Les Milandes, but she lost her fight in May 1968, when the property was auctioned off to pay longstanding debts.

That summer, Baker and her children moved to Monaco, where Princess Grace and the Red Cross helped her find a large villa near Monte Carlo. Baker resumed her international tours, often taking some or all of her children with her. In June 1973, she returned to New York City to give a series of sold-out concerts at Carnegie Hall. A few months later she suffered another heart attack and a stroke while on tour in Denmark. She was soon performing again, however, the need for financial security overcoming her desire to retire.

On April 8, 1975, Josephine Baker opened at the Bobino Theater in Paris with a new revue, entitled *Josephine.* The show was an instant hit, and Baker was once again the toast of Paris. She realized that it might be such a financial success that she could at last retire. Two days later those dreams were ended when Baker suffered a cerebral hemorrhage at her hotel and slipped into a deep coma. She died on April 12 and was buried three days later in a nationally televised ceremony at the Church of the Madeleine in Paris.

Actor Bill Cosby was born William Henry Cosby, Jr., on July 12, 1937, in Philadelphia. He grew up in an all-black housing project in that city's Germantown district. William Cosby, Sr., was a mess steward for the U.S. Navy and was away from home for months at a time. Mrs. Cosby, who worked as a cleaning woman, tried hard to protect Bill and his two younger brothers from their ghetto environment. She often read to them from the Bible and from the works of Mark Twain. Young Bill contributed to the meager family income by shining shoes and delivering groceries.

Bill Cosby's talents as a comedian were recognized at an early age. Inspired by TV comic Sid Caesar, young Cosby often entertained his classmates with made-up routines, and his sixth-grade teacher wrote on his report card that Bill was "an alert boy who would rather clown than study." Fortunately, the boy's brightness was also apparent and when he scored high on an IQ test in eighth grade he was assigned to a class for gifted students the following year at Germantown High School.

In high school Cosby excelled in athletics. He was captain of the track and football teams and also played basketball and baseball. His academic performance was unsatisfactory, however, and when he was told that he had to repeat 10th grade, he dropped out of school. Cosby worked for a while as a shoe repairman, then entered the U.S. Navy in 1956. During his four years in the navy, Cosby was trained as a physical therapist and worked at Bethesda Naval Hospital in Maryland. He also earned a high school equivalency diploma before his release in 1960.

Cosby enrolled at Temple University in Philadelphia in 1961 with the help of a track-and-field scholarship. He majored in physical education while participating on the university's track and football teams. During his sophomore year, Cosby began his career as a professional comedian when he was hired by a local coffeehouse to tend bar and tell jokes to customers for $5 a night. Later he was hired as a comedian at another night spot, the Underground, for $25 a night.

In the spring of 1962, Cosby took a leave of absence from Temple to entertain at the Gaslight Café, a coffeehouse in New York's Greenwich Village. Among his fellow performers was Woody Allen, then beginning his career as a stand-up comedian. Soon afterward Cosby severed his connection with Temple to become a full-time comic. As his reputation grew, he was invited to perform at leading clubs across the country and by 1963 he had become nationally known.

Almost from the beginning of his new career, Cosby had decided not to focus on racial material in order to reach a broad audience with his humor. "I want to play John Q. Public," he told an interviewer in 1963. His routines included anecdotes about everyday life, and he often made himself the butt of his own jokes, which he accented with humorous faces, sounds, and imper-sonations.

Following an appearance on Johnny Carson's *Tonight Show* in 1965, Cosby was asked by television producer Sheldon Leonard to do a screen test for a part in a new NBC-TV adventure series, *I Spy.* The test was successful, and Cosby was hired for the role of Alexander Scott, playing opposite Robert Culp as Kelly Robertson. Cosby thus became the first black actor to perform in a starring role in a nationally broadcast television series.

I Spy, with its realistic scenes and sly humor, was a popular show and ran for three years, from September 1965 to September 1968. It featured Culp and Cosby as a team of secret agents traveling undercover as a tennis player (Culp) and his trainer-companion (Cosby). Cosby won three consecutive Emmy awards for his performance in the show, in 1966, 1967, and 1968. Critics have since noted that Cosby's role was one of the most significant in the history of blacks on television, since it made a hero out of a mature, black secret service agent who was defending the United States around the world. Other black players often appeared in the series in nonstereotyped roles, including Cicely Tyson, Leslie Uggams, and Eartha Kitt.

Cosby returned to NBC-TV in the fall of 1969 with *The Bill Cosby Show*. The show was set in a high school located in a lower-middle-class neighborhood of Los Angeles and starred Cosby as a physical education teacher with a sense of humor who enjoyed helping others. The show ran for two seasons, until August 1971. That same year, Cosby made his first Hollywood film, costarring with Robert Culp in *Hickey and Boggs*, a movie about two private detectives in Los Angeles.

In February 1972, Cosby starred in *To All My Friends on Shore*, a made-for-television drama on CBS that he also wrote, scored, and produced. *The New Bill Cosby Show*, an hour-long comedy and variety program on CBS, premiered the following September. Cosby's guests included Sidney Poitier, Harry Belafonte, Peter Sellers, Lily Tomlin, and Tim Conway. Critics did not like the show, however, and it was dropped after one season.

During the 1972–73 season, Cosby also premiered another television program on CBS, a Saturday morning cartoon series called *Fat Albert and the Cosby Kids*. Cosby was the host and executive producer of the show, which featured a cast of humorous characters based on Cosby's boyhood friends. Cosby appeared at the beginning and end of each episode, which both entertained and offered a lesson in dealing with a specific childhood challenge—situations like losing a tooth, getting caught in telling a lie, or not being chosen for a team. *Fat Albert* was immensely popular, won numerous awards, and remained in production for 12 years; since 1984 it has been shown in reruns.

During the 1970s, Cosby was a frequent guest on the popular children's programs *Sesame Street* and *Electric Company*. In that decade, he also became a familiar television advertising personality, appearing in ads for a number of popular products. In 1974, Cosby appeared in another movie, *Uptown Saturday Night*, a comedy in which he costarred with Sidney Poitier, Harry Belafonte, Flip Wilson, and Richard Pryor. The following year Cosby and Poitier teamed up in another comedy, *Let's Do It Again*.

For several months in the fall of 1976, Cosby starred in *Cos*, a one-hour variety show for children on ABC-TV, but the show was unpopular and it soon went off the air. That same year, his fourth film, *Mother, Jugs and Speed*, was released, but it was not popular with either critics or audiences. Also in 1976, Cosby was awarded a doctorate in education by the University of Massachusetts, which gave him college credits for "life experience" and allowed him to fulfill practice teaching requirements by working as an instructor in prisons and appearing on *Sesame Street* and *Electric Company*.

In 1977, Cosby and Sidney Poitier were reunited in another film, *A Piece of the Action*, which also starred James Earl Jones. Although Cosby was praised for his performance, the movie itself received mixed reviews. Two years later, Cosby was part of an all-star cast that appeared in *California Suite*, a movie based on plays by Neil Simon. The film was a critical and popular success, although some reviewers criticized Cosby and costar Richard Pryor for engaging in a brawl scene, complaining that the fight was degrading to blacks and had racist overtones.

During the 1980s, Cosby appeared in several films, including *The Devil and Max Devlin* (1981), *Bill Cosby—Himself* (1983), and *Ghost Dad* (1989). In the fall of 1984, his new television program, *The Cosby Show*, premiered on NBC-TV. A situation comedy about a New York obstetrician, his lawyer wife, and their five children, the show was an immediate hit and ran for eight years.

In addition to a career as an actor and comic, Cosby is also well known as an author. His half-dozen books include *Fatherhood*, a collection of anecdotes and observations about being a father. (Cosby and his wife, Camille, whom he married in 1964, are the parents of five children.) *Fatherhood*, published in 1986, was a best-seller for more than a year and sold nearly 3 million hardcover copies. Cosby has also made a number of recordings of songs and comedy routines.

Bill Cosby has earned more money than any other entertainer in the world and makes tens of millions of dollars annually from his various endeavors. He and his family are eager to put that money to good use and have made substantial charitable contributions. In 1988, Cosby and his wife made headlines when they donated $20 million to Spelman College, a noted institution for black women in Atlanta. This is the largest contribution ever made to a black college.

KATHERINE DUNHAM

Dancer and choreographer
Katherine Dunham was born in Chicago, Illinois, on
June 22, 1909, the daughter of Albert Dunham, a
tailor, and his wife, Fanny. Katherine and her older
brother, Albert junior, lived with their parents in
suburban Glen Ellyn for several years. Following the
death of Fanny Dunham in 1914, the family moved to
a tenement on the South Side of Chicago. Albert

Dunham remarried several years later and opened a dry cleaning shop in Joliet, Illinois. Katherine grew up in Joliet, attending local schools with her brother.

Katherine began to take piano lessons at the age of 11, and by the time she entered high school she had become both a gifted athlete and a talented amateur dancer. She excelled in basketball and track and was active in the school's dancing group, the Terpsichorean Club. The first hint of her talent as an entertainer came in 1924, when she organized a cabaret performance to benefit Brown's Chapel, the local African Methodist Episcopal church. Performing a Ukrainian folk dance before an audience of 400, she was the star of the show.

In 1926, following her graduation from high school, Dunham enrolled in a local junior college. Her brother, Albert junior, was now attending the University of Chicago. When she graduated two years later, her brother helped her gain admission to the university and find a job at a nearby public library. On campus, Dunham took dancing lessons in addition to academic courses, and her ballet teacher encouraged her to pursue a career as a dancer.

In 1930, with the help of friends, Dunham opened a dance studio on Chicago's South Side. Soon she had assembled a troupe of dancers, which she named the Ballet Nègre. In 1931, the troupe appeared at Chicago's annual Beaux Arts Ball, where they performed a routine called "Negro Rhapsody." The performance was not a success, however, and students drifted away from the studio, which soon closed.

One day Dunham attended a university lecture by a cultural anthropologist who discussed the influence of African culture on contemporary America. She was surprised to learn that many dances had originated in Africa and began studying African culture. Encouraged by her ballet teacher, she also began incorporating African dance movements into her own routines.

In 1934, Dunham danced the lead role in *La Guiablesse*, a new ballet based on a Caribbean folktale, which was presented at the Chicago Opera House. In the audience at the first performance, which received enthusiastic reviews, was an executive of the Rosenwald Fund, a philanthropic organization. Dunham was encouraged to apply for a grant from the fund, which she received early in 1935 for the study of African dance in the Caribbean.

After several months of preparation, including studies with noted anthropology professor Melville J. Herskovits, Dunham headed for the West Indies. She spent several months in a Jamaican village named Accompong, where she studied a group called the Maroons. These were descendants of 17th-century African slaves brought to Jamaica by the Spanish. Dunham then traveled to Haiti, the world's first black republic, and immediately fell in love with the country. As she learned traditional dances of the Haitians, she became fascinated by Voodoo, the folk religion of the country, and was initiated into its practices.

Shortly after her return to the United States in the summer of 1936, Dunham received her bachelor's degree in anthropology from the University of Chicago. Although she was encouraged to do graduate work in anthropology, Dunham decided to pursue a career in dance. She resumed work with an ensemble of dancers under the tutelage of her old ballet teacher, Ludmila Speranzeva. News of her talent spread, and in early 1937 Dunham and her troupe performed for the first time in New York City, where audiences were captivated by her newly choreographed West Indian dances.

Back in Chicago, Dunham became active in the Negro Federal Theater Project and presented two dances that she had choreographed, *Ballet Fèdère* and *Biguine*. These dances marked the beginning of Dunham's career as a major force in black American dance. Dunham's work with the Federal Theater introduced her to John Pratt, a white Canadian set and costume designer. The two were married in 1939; many years later, in 1952, the couple adopted an orphan from Martinique whom they named Marie Christine.

With Pratt as her partner, Dunham established the Dunham Dance Company with a resident troupe of dancers that performed a broad repertoire. In the fall of 1939, the group moved to New York City, and Dunham immediately began choreographing a new show, *Tropics and Le Jazz Hot: From Haiti to Harlem.* The show debuted in the rented Windsor Theater on February 18, 1940, and made dance history. The audience went wild, and Dunham was hailed by critics as "the first pioneer of the Negro dance."

The success of Dunham's first New York show attracted the attention of the famous choreographer George Balanchine, who offered her the opportunity to collaborate with him on a new, all-black Broadway musical, *Cabin in the Sky*. The show was a big hit and played for five months to standing-room-only audiences in New York before going on a cross-country tour. When they reached Hollywood, the Dunham Dance Company made a movie short, *Carnival of Rhythm*, for Warner Brothers. This was the beginning of a successful film career for Dunham, who appeared in five more movies during the 1940s.

In 1941, Dunham created a new show called *Tropical Review*, which she took on tour for several years. By 1944, when the tour ended, Dunham realized that she could not go on dancing forever. Age and severe arthritis were taking their toll. In New York City in 1945, she opened the Katherine Dunham School of Dance, which she hoped would give "the Negro dance student the courage really to study, and a reason to do so." During its 10-year existence the school trained an entire generation of black dancers, including Eartha Kitt and Arthur Mitchell. Many famous actors also came to Dunham's school to learn techniques of body movement.

In 1946, Dunham published *Journey to Accompong*, an account of her trip to Jamaica more than a decade earlier. Later that year she and her husband put together a new show, *Bal Nègre*, with Pratt as set and costume designer and Dunham as choreographer and dancer. The review, which featured black dances from the Caribbean, Africa, Latin America, and the United States, was another hit for Dunham. Buoyed by this success, Dunham prepared for her first world tour.

The two-year tour began in Mexico in January 1948, where the Dunham Dance Company performed for six months to enthusiastic audiences. That summer they moved on to the major cities of Europe, where more acclaim greeted Dunham's dancing. Upon returning to New York City in 1950, the troupe introduced a new show, *Caribbean Rhapsody*. They then traveled to Latin America, where they spent several months in Brazil, Argentina, and Jamaica. After the tour, Dunham and her husband traveled to Haiti, where they lived for a while at a villa called Habitacion Leclerq.

During the 1950s, Dunham and her company continued their dance tours in the United States and abroad. In 1955, she introduced a new production, *Carnaval*, and later that year made her first tour of Australia and the Far East.

Increasingly bothered by physical ailments, Dunham realized by the fall of 1957, as the group concluded its Asian tour, that she could no longer continue her present pace. Dissolving the company, Dunham stayed behind in Japan to rest and began writing an autobiography. She completed the book following her return to the United States in 1958, and it was published a year later as *A Touch of Innocence*. Her third book, an account of her experiences in Haiti entitled *Island Possessed*, was published in 1969.

In 1961, Dunham and her husband tried to establish a resort at Habitation Leclerq, their Haitian home, but the attempt was unsuccessful and the couple were forced to leave Haiti for financial reasons. In 1962, they put together a new show, *Bamboche*, which enjoyed a brief success in New York City. Later that year Dunham was hired as the first black choreographer by the Metropolitan Opera House, but her dances for *Aïda* were rebuffed by critics and she was not invited to work on other productions there.

In 1965, Dunham was named artist-in-residence at Southern Illinois University, and she and her husband moved to the university's home city of Carbondale. That same year she traveled to Africa to help run the First World Festival of Negro Arts in Dakar, Senegal, and also choreographed works in Rome, Paris, and New York. Two years later, with the help of government and private grants, Dunham established the Performance Arts Training Center, a school for impoverished black youth in East St. Louis, Illinois, which she continues to direct.

Dunham lived in East St. Louis with her husband of 47 years, John Pratt, until his death in 1986. She has received numerous honors for her work, including the Albert Schweitzer Music Award in 1979, the Kennedy Center Honors in 1983, an honorary doctorate from Lincoln University in 1984, and the Scripps American Dance Festival Award in 1986.

LENA HORNE

Singer and actress Lena Horne was born on June 30, 1917, in Brooklyn, New York. Her family had been prominent for many years in civic and cultural affairs. When Lena was three years old, her father, a civil servant as well as a numbers runner and gambler, left home. While her mother, an actress, toured the East Coast, Lena was raised by various relatives in the South. One of them,

Dr. Frank Smith Horne, an uncle who lived in Georgia, was an educator who later became an adviser on race relations to President Franklin D. Roosevelt.

When Lena was 12, she returned to Brooklyn. She lived first with her grandmother and then with her mother and stepfather, and attended local schools. At 16, Horne left high school to help support her mother. She was hired as a chorus girl at the Cotton Club, a famous nightclub in Harlem, and during the next two years appeared there with well-known African American entertainers. In 1934, she made her debut on Broadway in the play *Dance with Your Gods*. A year later she left the Cotton Club to become a singer with Noble Sissle's orchestra and toured the East and Midwest. Using the name Helena Horne, she became the orchestra's temporary leader after Sissle was injured in an accident.

In January 1937, Horne married Louis J. Jones, a friend of her father's who was active in Democratic party politics in Pittsburgh. The couple had two children—Gail, born in 1937, and Teddy, born in 1940. Horne had intended to give up show business when she married, but her husband had a difficult time finding a job during the depression and she was forced to continue working. She sang at private parties in Pittsburgh and in 1938 made her screen debut in an all-black film, *The Duke Is Tops*. The following year she was one of the stars of a Broadway revue, *Blackbirds of 1939*.

Horne's husband resented her career, and the couple separated in 1940; they were divorced four years later. Horne returned to New York City in the fall of 1940 and was hired as a vocalist with Charlie Barnet's orchestra, becoming one of the first black performers to sing with an all-white band. She went on to make two hit recordings with Barnet, "Good for Nothing Joel" and "Haunted Town." In March 1941, she became a soloist at the Café Society Downtown Club in Greenwich Village, again billed as Helena Horne.

Three weeks after Horne opened at the club, the manager, Barney Josephson, sponsored a concert for her at Carnegie Hall. During her year at Café Society, which she later described as one of the happiest years of her life, Horne made recordings with a number of well-known jazz musicians, including Teddy Wilson (who then led the Café Society orchestra), Artie Shaw, and Henry Levine's Dixieland Jazz Group. She also made her first solo recordings for RCA Victor, including "I Gotta Right To Sing the Blues" and "Moanin' Low."

In February 1942, Horne left New York and moved to Los Angeles, where she joined Katherine Dunham's dancers and other black performers in a show at Little Troc, a Hollywood nightclub. She quickly became the most popular member of the show, and a scout from Metro-Goldwyn-Mayer arranged for her to have a screen test. Her singing so impressed executive Louis B. Mayer that he offered her a contract. Although Horne was not sure that she wanted to act in movies, friends urged her to accept the offer. Among them were Walter White, executive secretary of the National Association for the Advancement of Colored People (NAACP), and the bandleader Count Basie; both White and Basie believed that Horne could pave the way for other black actors in films.

Horne made her MGM debut in 1942 in the movie *Panama Hattie*, a musical by Cole Porter. The following year she costarred in the all-black musical *Cabin in the Sky*. Also in 1943, she was top star in another black musical, *Stormy Weather*. Horne had already sung the title song in her nightclub act and had recorded it, and it became the song most closely associated with her during her long career.

Cabin in the Sky and *Stormy Weather* established Horne as a film star, but she and the movie studios could not agree on subsequent roles for her. She refused to play stereotyped black characters, and as a light-complexioned African American she was neither "black" nor "white." As a kind of compromise, her subsequent film roles featured her in entertaining musical numbers that were inserted into movies but were unrelated to the main plot.

Despite this restriction in her roles, Horne was still a popular actress and was the favorite pinup girl of black soldiers during World War II. Horne made a major contribution to the war effort, touring army bases around the country to entertain troops. She was dismayed to find her audiences segregated, however, and was particularly upset when she came onstage during a performance at Fort Riley, Kansas, and discovered that German prisoners of war had been given better seats than black troops.

During the 1940s, Horne continued to work in nightclubs in addition to her film roles and armed forces shows. As the first black performer to appear at the Savoy Plaza Hotel and the Copacabana in New York City, she set box office records. Soon she was performing at top clubs in cities across the country, and she also appeared in London and Paris, where she quickly became a favorite. In 1948, *Life* magazine called her "the season's top nightclub attraction," and by 1952 she was earning as much as $12,500 a week.

Shortly after this, however, Horne's career began to decline. Over the years she had become involved in a number of political and social organizations, and some of them had been identified as having communist sympathies. In the early 1950s, there was strong anti-communist feeling in the United States, and Horne was blacklisted for her alleged connections to communism. Her friendship with the singer Paul Robeson, an open supporter of the Soviet Union, also contributed to her being blacklisted.

Horne fought back, denying that she was anything but a loyal American. By 1956, she was once again performing for audiences, making a guest appearance in the movie *Meet Me in Las Vegas* and appearing on popular TV shows hosted by Ed Sullivan, Steve Allen, and Perry Como. Horne also recorded new songs for RCA Victor. One of her first LPs (long-playing records) for RCA, *Lena Horne at the Waldorf-Astoria*, became the largest-selling album by a female performer in the company's history. In 1957, Horne starred in the Broadway musical *Jamaica*; although critics were lukewarm about the show they lauded her performance, and *Jamaica* lasted for 555 performances.

During the 1960s, Horne was one of the most prominent black celebrities who supported the civil rights movement. She traveled throughout the South, singing and speaking at rallies, and she added songs with civil rights themes to her repertoire. She also participated in meetings of black leaders with government officials. During these years Horne starred in several television specials and also published her autobiography, *Lena* (1965).

In 1970–71, Horne lost several of those closest to her. First her father died, and then her son succumbed to a kidney ailment. In 1971, her second husband, Lennie Hayton, also died. She had married Hayton, a musical director at MGM, in 1944, and he had become her conductor and arranger.

In the face of these multiple tragedies, Horne lost interest in her work for a while. Gradually she resumed her tours of theaters and nightclubs throughout the country, appearing with fellow stars Alan King, Tony Bennett, and Count Basie. In 1974, she appeared as Glinda the Good Witch in the film *The Wiz*, an all-black version of *The Wizard of Oz*.

Horne's one-woman show, *Lena Horne: The Lady and Her Music*, was an instant hit when it opened in New York in 1981. Nearly all of its 333 performances sold out, and Horne received a number of awards, including the Handel Medallion, New York City's highest cultural award, and the Emergence Award from the Dance Theatre of Harlem. She was also honored by the Duke Ellington School of the Arts in Washington, D.C., which established a scholarship in her name. Horne later took the show on tour across the United States and to London, where audiences were uniformly enthusiastic.

Horne has received other awards for her work as a performer and civil rights activist. In 1979, she was awarded an honorary doctor of laws degree from Howard University in Washington, D.C. Three years later she received the Spingarn Medal, given annually by the NAACP in recognition of high achievement by a black American. In December 1984, Horne was one of five recipients of the annual Kennedy Center Honors in Washington, D.C. She has also received the Governor's Arts Award from New York State and the Paul Robeson Award from Actors' Equity.

Actor Sidney Poitier was born on February 20, 1927, in Miami, Florida. His parents, farmers in the Bahamas, had come to Miami to sell their crop of tomatoes, and their seventh child was born there prematurely. Several weeks later the three Poitiers returned to their home on Cat Island, where Sidney spent the first ten years of his life.

In 1937, worsening economic conditions led the Poitiers to move to Nassau, the capital city of the Bahamas. Their lives did not improve, however, and they lived in extreme poverty. The only bright spot in Sidney's life was the movies, which he had discovered soon after his arrival in Nassau. He often skipped school, and by his early teens, pranks and more serious misbehavior were causing his parents concern. In January 1943, they sent him to Miami to live with his oldest brother, Cyril, and his wife.

In Miami, Sidney Poitier experienced severe racial discrimination for the first time. He also discovered that there were few employment opportunities for him, since he had little education. After a few months of working at a series of menial jobs in the racially tense atmosphere of the South, Poitier decided to leave. Working his way north, he reached New York City in the summer of 1943.

Poitier was immediately captivated by New York, although his first months there were far from comfortable. He worked for a while as a dishwasher and often slept outdoors. As winter approached, Poitier experienced cold weather for the first time. With no warm clothing and no place to stay, he decided to join the U.S. Army. Lying about his age, he was inducted in November 1943 and served for a year as an orderly in a mental hospital in Northport, New York.

Dismissed from the service in December 1944, a more mature Poitier returned to New York City determined to make a career for himself. With severance pay from the army, Poitier rented a room in Harlem and found a job as a dishwasher. One day in 1945, he read an article in the *Amsterdam News*, a black newspaper, about the American Negro Theatre, which was looking for new actors. On a whim, Poitier decided to audition but was turned aside by the group's manager, Frederick O'Neal, because of his thick West Indian accent and also because he was barely literate.

Poitier responded by embarking upon a self-improvement program. He bought a radio and every evening spent hours imitating voices that he heard on broadcasts. He also improved his literacy skills by reading a newspaper carefully every day. In April 1946, Poitier returned to the American Negro Theatre for another audition. This time he was given a three-month trial admission to the school run by the group.

Poitier worked as a packer in a shirt factory during the day while he attended acting classes at night. At the end of the trial period, Poitier was asked to leave because of insufficient progress, but he won a three-month extension by agreeing to serve without pay as the theater janitor. The determined Poitier slowly made progress, and he became the understudy for a young actor in the troupe named Harry Belafonte in a play called *Days of Our Youth*. One night when Belafonte was ill, Poitier assumed his role during a rehearsal. In the audience was James Light, a prominent director, who was so impressed by Poitier that he offered him a part in an all-black

Broadway production of the ancient Greek comedy *Lysistrata*.

Although the production was a failure, critics praised Poitier for his performance, and the American Negro Theatre offered him a job as an understudy in their touring show, *Anna Lucasta*. Poitier toured with the show for three years, and by the time it ended in 1949 he had learned to act and to work with a drama company. Back in New York, he won an audition for a major role in the film *No Way Out*, in which he played a young doctor who was the victim of racial prejudice. Critics praised Poitier for his performance in the film, which was released in 1950.

Poitier's next project was the film version of Alan Paton's novel *Cry, the Beloved Country*, a story of racial segregation in South Africa. The movie was made in that country, and Poitier, forced because of his color to stay near the black shantytowns of Johannesburg, got a close look at the pain and suffering of racial oppression. Released in 1951, Poitier's second film was also a critical success.

That same year Poitier married Juanita Hardy, a model and dancer, and a year later their first daughter was born. Poitier and his wife had three more daughters before their divorce in the 1970s. Poitier married his second wife, an actress named Joanna Shimkus, in 1976; they are the parents of two daughters.

Despite the success of his first two films, Poitier found it difficult to find other parts during the early 1950s. Finally, he was offered a leading role in the

1955 movie *Blackboard Jungle*, in which he played a rebellious teenager. The film was a great commercial success and Poitier was acclaimed for his performance. He made other films in quick succession, including *Edge of the City, Something of Value, Mark of the Hawk*, and *Band of Angels*, and also appeared in a television drama for the first time. His next film, *The Defiant Ones*, released in 1958, earned Poitier his first Academy Award nomination for Best Actor.

In 1959, Poitier starred as Porgy in the movie version of George Gershwin's musical *Porgy and Bess*, lip-synching the songs. Poitier was criticized for making this film, which many blacks felt was denigrating to their race. The following year, however, he received cheers from both blacks and whites for his performance in the Broadway production of *A Raisin in the Sun*, a play about a poor black family in Chicago. In 1961, he also starred in the film version. During the early 1960s, Poitier made four other movies: *All the Young Men*, in which he played a sergeant in the Korean War; *Paris Blues*, about jazz musicians; *Pressure Point*, in which he played a prison psychiatrist; and *Lilies of the Field*, about a young drifter who befriends a group of nuns in the American Southwest.

Lilies of the Field won Poitier an Oscar as Best Actor in the spring of 1964—the first time a black man had won the award. Following this victory, Poitier made five more films in quick succession—*The Bedford Incident, The Long Ships, The Slender Thread, Duel at Diablo*, and *A Patch of Blue*—which were moderately successful. Poitier had a major hit in the 1967 film *To Sir with Love*, in which he played a schoolteacher in the London slums. That year a Gallup Poll named him the most popular movie star in America.

Poitier made two more hit films in 1967: *Guess Who's Coming to Dinner?* in which he plays the fiancé of a white woman, and *In the Heat of the Night*, co-starring Poitier as a detective arrested for murder in a small southern town. Both movies were nominated for an Academy Award as Best Picture of the Year, and *In the Heat of the Night* received the Oscar.

By this time, Poitier had decided to create his own projects rather than waiting for roles to be offered to him. His first attempt in this direction was a low-budget film called *For Love of Ivy* (1968), about the strivings of a young black woman; Poitier developed the idea for the script, helped finance the picture, and costarred. During the early 1970s, however, his career fell into what he later termed a "twilight zone." So-called black-exploitation movies were on the rise, featuring street life, and there was little demand for the gentler "crossover films," those appealing to both black and white audiences, that Poitier had acted in and sometimes directed during these years.

Poitier's career took an upturn in 1975 with the box office success of *Uptown Saturday Night*, a comedy he directed and in which he costarred with Bill Cosby, Harry Belafonte, and Richard Pryor. A sequel, *Let's Do It Again*, was released the following year and was also a commercial success, as was *A Piece of the Action*, another comedy released in 1977.

During the next decade Poitier was absent from the screen as an actor, although he directed several successful pictures, including *Fast Forward* (1985). In 1987, he returned to film acting in *Little Nikita* and has appeared in several other films in recent years. Poitier's autobiography, *This Life*, was published in 1980.

PAUL ROBESON

Singer and actor Paul Leroy Robeson was born on April 9, 1898, in Princeton, New Jersey, where his father, William, was the pastor of a black church. Paul was the youngest of eight children. His mother, Anna Robeson, was a schoolteacher of African, Indian, and English ancestry. William Robeson had escaped from slavery at the age of fifteen, fought in the Union Army during the Civil War, and then worked his way through Lincoln University, where he trained to become a minister.

When Paul Robeson was six years old, his mother died from burns suffered in a household accident. By this time, Paul was the only child still living at home, and he and his father moved to Westfield, New Jersey, where they lived for a while. Then William Robeson was appointed pastor of the St. Thomas African Methodist Episcopal Zion Church in Somerville, another New Jersey town, and father and son resettled there.

Paul Robeson attended local schools in Somerville and was an excellent student. During his senior year in high school, he scored highest in a competitive examination for a four-year scholarship to Rutgers College (later Rutgers University). In the fall of 1915, several months after his high school graduation, he entered Rutgers, becoming the first member of his family to attend a white college. At Rutgers he was the only black student then enrolled, and only the third black student in the college's 149-year history.

Despite his uniqueness, Robeson was a popular student at Rutgers. Standing six feet three inches and weighing 240 pounds, Robeson was a handsome and imposing figure with a deep voice, and he impressed everyone who met him. He won the freshman prize for oratory and the sophomore and junior prizes for extemporaneous speaking. He also excelled in athletics and earned an impressive 12 varsity letters in four sports—football, baseball, basketball, and track. He was named an All-American end in 1917 and 1918 and won the admiration of white teammates who had earlier threatened to quit the football team if he was allowed to play.

Robeson participated in a number of other college activities while compiling an outstanding academic record and working throughout his four years at Rutgers at a series of menial jobs to pay for expenses. He was elected to Phi Beta Kappa, the academic honor society, in his junior year, and the following year was named to another honor society, Cap and Skull. He was selected to give the commencement address at his graduation in 1919.

Robeson then moved to Harlem, a black neighborhood in New York City, and in 1920 was admitted to the Columbia University Law School. He paid for his studies by playing professional football on weekends. During his first year at Columbia, a new friend named Eslanda Goode encouraged him to launch a career as an actor. Robeson first appeared in an amateur production at the Harlem YMCA and made his professional debut at the Lafayette Theatre in 1921. That same year he married Goode, a graduate student in chemistry at Columbia.

Robeson continued his law studies while he appeared on Broadway and also toured England briefly. In 1923, he received his law degree from Columbia, was admitted to the bar, and was hired by a law firm headed by a well-known Rutgers graduate. Robeson quickly realized that there would be few opportunities for him in an all-white firm, and the lure of the theater proved irresistible. By 1924, he had abandoned a career as a lawyer and joined the Provincetown Players, an experimental acting troupe based in Greenwich Village. The well-known playwright Eugene O'Neill was associated with the troupe, and in May 1924 Robeson starred in two O'Neill plays presented at the Provincetown (Massachusetts) Playhouse: *The Emperor Jones* and *All God's Chillun Got Wings.* Reviewers were enthusiastic, and Robeson became particularly celebrated for his portrayal of Brutus Jones, the black dictator of a West Indian island in *The Emperor Jones.*

In 1925, Robeson and a friend, composer and pianist Lawrence Brown, presented a concert of Negro spirituals and folk songs in New York City. Robeson's performance impressed audience and critics alike, and during 1925–26, Robeson and Brown toured the United States, Great Britain, and Europe. Robeson had an aptitude for languages—he eventually mastered more than twenty—and he learned the folk songs of many nations in their original tongues.

During the next 15 years, Robeson gave numerous concerts at home and abroad. He also performed as a singer and actor on the radio and stage and in films, and made more than 300 recordings. His most notable roles included Joe in *Show Boat*, singing "Ole Man River," and the lead in *Othello*. Robeson first played Othello in London in 1930; 13 years later he starred in a highly acclaimed Broadway production of Shakespeare's play and made theater history as the first black lead with a white supporting cast. In 1959, Robeson was again hailed when he starred in a performance of Othello in Shakespeare's home village, Stratford-on-Avon, England.

Robeson also appeared in celebrated film versions of *The Emperor Jones* (1933) and *Show Boat* (1936), and was praised for his work in other movies during the 1930s and early 1940s. During World War II, he withdrew from film acting, however, explaining that "The industry is not prepared to permit me to portray the life or express the living interests, hopes, and aspirations of the struggling people from whom I come."

During his first visit to the Soviet Union in 1934, Robeson had been impressed by the communist system and what he believed was its lack of social and racial discrimination. He became fluent in the Russian language and was a frequent visitor to the USSR, where he became a popular performer. At one point Robeson declared that he loved Russia more than any other country and sent his only child, Paul junior, to school there.

Robeson became a prominent supporter of many left-wing causes at home and abroad, including those in Great Britain, Spain, and West Africa, and in the 1930s he spent much of his time abroad. When he returned with his family to the United States in 1939, he observed that the country's racial climate seemed to have improved. During World War II, Robeson continued his support of antifascist groups, often giving benefit concerts to raise money for refugees.

After the war, as tensions increased between the United States and the Soviet Union, Robeson's

popularity in his home country declined. He was ac-
cused of being a communist and was denounced in
newspapers and magazines as a supporter of the
USSR. He was no longer in demand as a concert
performer and actor, and his recordings were
withdrawn from stores. Pressure was even placed upon
Rutgers University to withdraw Robeson's name from
alumni rolls and athletic records and to rescind an
honorary degree that the college had given him.

In the face of these attacks, Robeson reaffirmed his
support for the socialist practices of the Soviet Union,
"which in one generation has raised our people to the
full dignity of mankind." In 1950, the U.S. State
Department demanded that Robeson surrender his
passport and denied him the right to travel abroad
unless he signed a loyalty oath. For the next eight
years, Robeson fought this ban through a series of
lawsuits in federal courts. During this time he earned
virtually no money; his only concert appearances were
before small radical groups. His stature in America
was further diminished in 1952, when the Soviet
Union awarded him the Stalin Peace Prize.

By 1958, when Robeson won his battle with the
State Department and recovered his passport, anti-
communist feeling in the United States had lessened
somewhat, and he gave what was billed as a "farewell
concert" that year in New York City's Carnegie Hall.
After making a short tour of the West Coast and
recording an album, he left the United States and lived
abroad for five years. In 1959, while traveling in Russia, he was hospitalized for circulatory and other ail-

ments. He spent the next few years in and out of hospitals in Eastern Europe and England but never fully regained his health.

In 1963, Robeson and his wife returned to the United States. Robeson announced his retirement from the stage and all public affairs—he had not sung in public since 1961—and went into seclusion. Following the death of his wife in December 1965, Robeson moved to Philadelphia to live with a sister.

During the 1970s, many of Robeson's recordings were reissued and in 1973 he was honored on his 75th birthday by a gala at Carnegie Hall. Paying tribute to Robeson on this occasion were leading black entertainers and civil rights leaders, including Harry Belafonte, Sidney Poitier, and Coretta Scott King. Robeson was too ill to attend, but a tape-recorded message from him was played at the event. He died on January 23, 1976, in Philadelphia.

Alvin Ailey

Haskings, James. *Black Dance in America.* New York: HarperCollins, 1990.

Mazo, Joseph H. *The Alvin Ailey American Dance Theater.* New York: Morrow, 1978.

Probosz, Kathilyn Solomon. *Alvin Ailey, Jr.* New York: Bantam Skylark, 1991.

Marian Anderson

Anderson, Marian. *My Lord, What a Morning.* New York: Viking, 1956.

Sims, Janet L. *Marian Anderson: An Annotated Bibliography and Discography.* Westport, CT: Greenwood Press, 1981.

Tedards, Anne. *Marian Anderson.* New York: Chelsea House, 1988.

Josephine Baker

Papich, Stephen. *Remembering Josephine.* Indianapolis: Bobbs-Merrill, 1976.

Rose, Phyllis. *Jazz Cleopatra: Josephine Baker in Her Time.* New York: Doubleday, 1989.

Schroeder, Alan. *Josephine Baker.* New York: Chelsea House, 1991.

Bill Cosby

Adams, Barbara Johnston. *The Picture Life of Bill Cosby.* New York: Watts, 1986.

Cosby, Bill. *Fatherhood.* New York: Doubleday, 1986.

Haskins, Jim. *Bill Cosby: America's Most Famous Father.* Houston: Walker, 1988.

Herbert, Solomon J., and George H. Hill. *Bill Cosby.* New York: Chelsea House, 1992.

Katherine Dunham

Dominy, Jeannine. *Katherine Dunham.* New York: Chelsea House, 1992.

Dunham, Katherine. *Dances of Haiti.* Los Angeles: Center for Afro-American Studies, University of California, Los Angeles, 1983.

———. *A Touch of Innocence.* New York: Books for Libraries, 1980.

Lena Horne

Buckley, Gail Lumet. *The Hornes: An American Family.* New York: Knopf, 1986.

Lanker, Brian. *I Dream a World: Portraits of Black Women Who Changed America.* New York: Stewart, Tabori and Chang, 1989.

Palmer, Leslie. *Lena Horne.* New York: Chelsea House, 1989.

Sidney Poitier

Bergman, Carol. *Sidney Poitier.* New York: Chelsea House, 1988.

Keyser, Lester J. *The Cinema of Sidney Poitier.* New York: Barnes, 1980.

Poitier, Sidney. *This Life.* New York: Ballantine/Knopf, 1980.

Paul Robeson

Ehrlich, Scott. *Paul Robeson.* New York: Chelsea House, 1988.

Robeson, Paul. *Here I Stand.* Boston: Beacon Press, 1971.

Robeson, Susan. *The Whole World in His Hands.* Secaucus, NJ: Citadel Press, 1981.

❧ INDEX ❧

❧ PICTURE CREDITS ❧

RICHARD RENNERT has edited the nearly 100 volumes in Chelsea House's award-winning BLACK AMERICANS OF ACHIEVEMENT series, which tells the stories of black men and women who have helped shape the course of modern history. He is also the author of several sports biographies, including *Henry Aaron*, *Jesse Owens*, and *Jackie Robinson*. He is a graduate of Haverford College in Haverford, Pennsylvania.